The Dos & Don'ts Of A Committed Relationship

The Dos & Don'ts Of A Committed Relationship

By Sirron V. Kyles

An Informative Insight Into Committed Relationships

Copyright ©2015
Author Sirron V. Kyles

Bar Code: 7878579468827
ISBN: 10: 069246753X
ISBN: 13: 978-0-692-46753-4

Cover By Sirron 12
Illustrations Ariadna Pérez Hernández

All Rights Reserved. No part of this book may be reproduced in any form, by either electronic or mechanical means, including information storage or retrieval systems, without permission in writing from the publisher. The exception is in reviews that quote brief passages.

Published & Printed In The USA
Publish 2015 HousTone Publishing
PO Box 8305 Houston, Texas 77288 USA

info@houstonepublishing.com * www.houstonepublishing.com
PH-713-866-4006 Ext. 2 * Fax-713-866-4006

Table of Content

About The Author 7
Author's Preface 9
Tolerance 13
Honesty 19
Communication 25
Commitment 29
Temptation 33
Finances 37
Faith 41
Family 47
Friends 51
Sex 55
Politics 61
Conclusion 63
Contributors Research Sources 65
About Notes-Partners Relationship Log 67
Start Getting Closer Leave Notes Below 70

About The Author

Sirron V. Kyles was born in Texas and is best known as the creator of the Bob Marley Festival Tour. One of his many skill sets, he is a Visual Communication Creative Specialist who focuses on Art Décor Corporate & Individual Branding, Photography and Graphic Design. His education consists of certificates from Rice University, Lee Jr. College, San Jose State and degrees from Houston Community Colleges and the Columbia School of Broadcasting. According to Sirron, they each one helped him greatly in writing this book.

He was honorably discharged from the US Navy, which included three tours in Vietnam as a member of the Special Services. In high school he was a member of the ROTC and served on the Houston City Honor Guard, Color Guard and Drill Team, which he feels was very important in helping him establish discipline early in his life. Sirron also played basketball in the Navy, high school, collage and professionally (mostly in the ABA) and was a member of the swim team.

Sirron, said, "I have been involved in many committed relationships over the years, and always considered that I was popular with women."

"Those experiences provided a great deal of insight into the content of this book and the different points of understanding relationships that I may not have been aware of without the time I spent with the women I shared my life with."

Sirron has published several articles and other books that he either authored or coauthored.

Author's Preface

"The reason for writing this book was to share personal information, experiences and solutions from those who are now working through committed relationships, along with research and conversations with others who also have been in committed relationships. When making the decision to enter into a commitment with another person, it should never be taken lightly or made hastily. It is too serious of an undertaking to be based solely on emotions. Most of us would not marry another person without giving it serious consideration; why would you think of making a similar type of commitment without giving it the same amount of common sense reflection?"

To me, the most important way to start the conversation about the dos and don'ts of a committed relationship is to say that you don't have to believe everything you read in this book, but you might learn something if you do. Take this advice as just relationship information. Everyone's relationship is different and what matters to one person may not be important to another. Still, there are some general dos and don'ts outlined in chapters of this book that may prove very valuable when considering whether or not to enter a committed relationship.

There's always an exception to the rule. For example, things you shouldn't tell your partner:

"My mother thinks you're getting fat."

Or

"Actually, I think Scarlett Johansson/Chris Hemsworth/Tyra Banks/ Chris Evans/ Diego Boneta/Kate Upton/Denzel Washington/Sofia Vergara is way, way hotter than you."

You should use common sense concerning things that harm the relationship. Both parties should discuss past relationships. It may create doubt in their relationship during the beginning, until they get to know each other, but I feel it is best to start with a clean slate.

Tolerance, honesty, communication, sex, faith, commitment, family, temptation, politics, finances and friends all influence how long and strong a committed relationship will be. I know from personal experience that each of them influenced how my committed relationships transpired. I'm sad to say that 75% of those relationships ended as a result of me deciding to let don'ts influence my decisions and clearly not just the fault of the wonderful ladies that chose to make commitments with me - just saying.

There are general dos and don'ts that you can use as guidance in this book, no matter what stage your relationship is in. I only wish I had read a book like this earlier in life. I am sure I would have made wiser decisions in some of my past relationships, but as a result of writing this book, I will make better decisions in future relationships.

Tolerance

Chapter 1

Tolerance

Tolerance, in reference to this chapter, is about tolerating (or forgiving) actions or poor judgments of a partner they may not agree with in order to maintain the committed relationship. For couples that have been married for many years, one thing that keeps them together is tolerance and forgiveness of their partner's errors in judgments. The other reasons they chose to show tolerance may have something to do with their fear of being alone or the loss of security they have with their partner.

Intolerance is a character flaw in people with self-righteous personalities that may stem from how they were brought up or if they were mistreated as a child.

In her article "Tolerance, An Important Relationship Virtue," Sonja Ridden states:

"How would it be if you lost the occasional battle? I'd like to challenge you to ask yourself why you feel the way you do each time intolerance strikes. If you do this chances are that you'll find your feelings have little to do with the current circumstance but are deeply rooted in an earlier time of your life."

To make a commitment last, you must first understand the Dos and Don'ts of Tolerance.

As a child, were you told not to voice your opinion and do what ever your parents requested? Were you were teased and bullied? Did you observe things done by people you respected that you knew were wrong, but never spoke of them? There may have been many times you kept quiet when you wanted to say things to someone you liked, just to keep from rocking the boat. At some point in your life, you made the decision that no one would get away with anything you felt was wrong.

If you want to honor the commitment and make it work, Don't, use your past to make intolerant decisions today, especially when it comes to forgiving your partner for their mistakes. Try to understand your intolerant behavior. If you don't, you can bet that it will make your life and the life of your love ones miserable. Work on discovering your tolerance level. If it is low, release those emotions and the following points will be easier to implement. Do let others occasionally enjoy the pleasure of being right. Choose your arguments wisely.

Don't: Focus on minor disagreements.

Give others the benefit of the doubt. Remember that people are imperfect, including you. Don't think that you may not always be right, but you are never wrong because you could be. Do practice tolerance. It is a vital key in maintaining a healthy, long-term relationship. Relationship conflicts occur when people don't listen to each other.

There are four fundamentals that lead to a happy relationship. They are compassion, which brings about caring; understanding, which leads to knowing; tolerance, which shows respect and empathy, which results in connection. In the end, it is all about love.

Do: Keep calm.

It is important that both partners recognize the other person's sensitivities and explain those sensitivities to each other because each person has different a points of view, but can learn from each other if they share those points. Angry partners must calm down and acknowledge their differences while trying to understand the cause of the disagreement and coming up with a solution or compromise so they can both move forward.

I have to acknowledge my own intolerance during past committed relationships. I was often annoyed at the lack of discipline I saw in my partners, which I believed stemmed from my military background.

Due to my experiences and focus on running a business, I had a tendency to nag and underestimate the wisdom of my partners in many instances. Looking back, I can easily recognize my errors that caused the relationships to fail. I can frankly state that although the relationships failed, it was not always just my fault, but I am not the same person as result of what I learned from my partners.

Honesty

Ariadna Pérez Hernández

Chapter 2

Honesty

You have to be able to trust your partner, and you earn that trust by being honest yourself. Ground rules should be established at the beginning of the relationship detailing what each person will share about their past, good and bad. Many relations are doomed from the start because of partners sharing things from their past that may not seem like much to them, but may be seen as negative by their partner. You should get to know your partner before sharing things like how many people you have dated or slept with or, for that matter, how bad your last relationship ended, your dislike for their parents, etc.

Don't: Lie to your partner.

If you lie to your partner, you're saying that you're fine with them lying to you as well, but only in the same circumstances. Keeping a surprise party secret is not the same as your partner sleeping with your best buddy and lying about it. But if you keep a secret from your partner, you better be comfortable with the idea of them keeping a similar type of secret from you. If you're not, you need to seriously think about why you're keeping the secret and why you think what you're doing might hurt or anger your partner.

From the section "Truth and Honesty in Our Relationship, Telling The Truth" in *Straight from the Heart* by Layne and Paul Cutright:

"Truth is difficult for many of us. We all engage in a bit of self-deception in our lives. There are things about ourselves that we have not been able to examine or accept. We have difficulty in admitting our flaws - even to ourselves, much more so to our partners."

Sometimes we guard our intimate feelings because we have been hurt in the past when we tried to share them with others, so trust is difficult for us.

For example, if you and your partner are feeling unloved and lonely, but you try to cover it up by saying that everything is fine, you will continue to feel isolated. Our commitment to a relationship means that we have decided to open ourselves up to another person, flaws and all. Deceiving our partner impedes the intimacy of the relationship.

A relationship has the potential to provide a healthy way to come to terms with our issues, both personal and interpersonal. Accepting the truth and talking about it can free us from pain and set the stage for a healthier future.

When we share our fears within the context of our partner's love, understanding and acceptance, the fears dissipate. The issues we have been holding onto alone for so long lose their power when they are shared with someone who loves us.

Telling the truth can bring down the barriers that isolate us from our partners. It can lead to a new level of self-acceptance and authenticity in our own lives and this leads to a stronger level of commitment and intimacy in our relationship. The truth can make us whole and set us free.

Here are some guidelines for telling the truth:

1. Understand what you intend to do when you communicate.

This calls for an honest look at your motivations. If you intend to heal, clarify or deepen the sense of intimacy within the relationship, your intention will probably lead to these results. If, on the other hand, you want to make yourself look good and your partner look bad, or if you want to hurt your partner, then distrust will be the result.

2. Assess how well your partner can handle the truth.

There are times when your partner may not be ready to have heartfelt discussions. One clue is when they continually reject, or are unable to hear, your attempts at increased closeness.

If your partner tends to become defensive, if there is a history of fighting when serious issues are discussed, if your partner is unable to honor your personal information and can't keep a secret or if there is a history of betrayal - it might be best to practice telling the truth with another person without your partner. When you feel comfortable telling the truth and trusting someone, it will be time to engage in heartfelt talks with your partner.

Some people prefer to start a solo process with a therapist since they are trained to listen nonjudgmentally and are less likely to take things personally. Understand your own fears about telling the truth

Communicating in an honest and truthful way makes you vulnerable. You may fear getting hurt or hurting your partner's feelings. You may feel that you will be misunderstood or that your partner will judge you. Our fears are based on past experiences and reside within us. They are often unrealistic. The higher goal is to communicate truthfully with your partner in order to have a more satisfying relationship and this means having the courage to confront your fears.

3. Accept that your partner does not have to agree with you.

Many of us are afraid of having intimate talks with our partners unless they agree with everything we say. This does not lead to intimacy, which involves a sharing and accepting our differences. It does control struggles and isolates us from our partners. Accept, even treasure, your partner's individuality.

Two people can be right at the same time in a relationship - it's just a matter of two different interpretations of the same events. Intimacy occurs between two complete individuals when each of them honors their partner's way of looking at the world.

It's not just big lies, though. Even little ones can cause problems. No matter how new the relationship is or how much you want them to like you, don't pretend to like things you really can't stand. When you're discovered – and you will – they're going to be hurt that you lied and they're going to see that you're not the person you said you were. And if you lied about that, what else have you lied about?

Dos: It's not just honesty; it's consistency. Be yourself, and trust that your partner likes you. It's a pretty shaky foundation when your relationship is based on a pack of half-truths. Hold yourself to the same standards you hold your partner to. At least then you will never be the hypocrite.

Communication

Ariadna Pérez Hernández

Chapter 3

Communication

Communication is one of the most important aspects of a committed relationship, but you don't always have to tell your partner everything – as I stated previously. At the same time, you don't get to know each other without communication, no matter how nice other aspects of your relationship are. You don't build something that will last if you don't know your partner. Communication is critical in creating a truly long-lasting relationship between two partners; without it, the relationship is doomed to fail.

However, what you communicate is also very important. You can get through almost anything with enough communication. When you have personal issues that are distracting you, communicating those issues with your partner is crucial. In most cases, as the old saying goes, two heads are better than one. You don't build something that will last if you don't know your partner. Knowing your partner well can even improve your sex life. Better communication is just talking, not fighting. Explore Notes-Partners Relationship Log, a perfect way to commutate intimately at the end of this book.

Getting comfortable with communicating about sex may translate to benefits in the bedroom — especially if the lines of communication are open during the act. New research finds that comfort with sexual communication is directly linked to sexual satisfaction. People who are more comfortable talking about sex are also more likely to apply their discussions during sex.

Nonetheless, that doesn't fully explain why the sexually chatty are happier with their erotic lives.

"Even if you just have a little bit of anxiety about the communication, that affects whether you're communicating or not, but it also directly affected their satisfaction," said Elizabeth Babin, a study researcher and expert on health communication at Cleveland State University in Ohio.

Don't: Meet with your ex.

It should only be done to finalize business left over from the relationship or involving kids, it should not be a problem since all partners get jealous when it comes to exes. Even if you tell your partner about your intentions first, there is always a trust issues when it comes to exes.

Do: Communicate honestly.

Your partner may still be concerned with the meeting, but because of the communication regarding its non-social status that you discussed in advance, and because you both agree on the importance of the meeting, it should not be a problem.

It's not like sneaking around behind their back; they know who you're seeing and why. Tell them what they need to know for comfort and let them tell you about any concerns they may have to help ease any jealous tendencies. Honesty and communication means your partner knows they can believe you and they know you'll listen to them and hear their pain. There aren't a whole lot of things you can do wrong when it comes to communication as long as you're doing it honestly. If you're not, any problem starts off twice as hard because you've got nowhere to start.

Commitment

Ariadna Pérez Hernández

Chapter 4

Commitment

My feeling is that everyone understands the definition of commitment. I will say that if you decide to enter into a committed relationship, it should be done using not only your emotions, but also logic, while understanding that you want to enjoy your life with another person for an extended period of time. Just Saying.

Commitment can mean all kinds of things. It'll come up in most relationships the moment you have to make some gesture or explicitly say that you are committed to them or that you love them. This is the only commitment that matters and it is the contract of a committed relationship. It might arise from meeting their parents, agreeing to be exclusive to one another, agreeing on relationship rules (like monogamy), etc.

Do: Keep the commitment.

The important thing is that once you've made a relationship commitment, you keep it and be there for your partner when they need you.

Do: Explain why.

Obviously, sometimes things happen that may cause you to break minor commitments, but if you're going to break one, you'd better be prepared to explain why to your partner.

Even if you know they'll understand, it's only fair to let them know what's going on and even better if you can discuss it and make sure it's okay after you break even a minor commitment. So make a consorted effort to meet with or call them, depending on the severity of the breach. Don't text; it's not personal enough and does not show how you truly feel about breaking the commitment.

Don't: Cheat.

Needless to say, if you and your partner have committed to each other and you're unfaithful, you've got a lot of explaining to do. In most cases, it will not matter what you say because you've broken the trust you had with your partner.

You can't expect things to go back to the way they were before. If they are considering giving you a second chance, you're going to have to work for it – and you can't get off with an expensive gesture.

If you're not up for making and keeping your commitments with this person, it's time to rethink the relationship because more than likely they are. Remember, you are giving your word when you make a commitment, especially in a relationship. Your word should mean a great deal to you. It is a promise you make to yourself and the other person.

Temptation

Ariadna Pérez Hernández

Chapter 5

Temptation

It happens to almost everyone. You meet someone by chance and they're really friendly and funny. You may have had a couple of drinks and you see a great looking person that catches your eye, forgetting for a moment that you're with a committed partner. You just stare…

However it happens, you have to stop and think when you're faced with temptation and the wandering eye. Is it worth it, if you care about your partner? Probably not!

Don't: Hurt your partner with it.

Some people might think that part of honesty and communication is telling their partner about the all of the little temptations and straying thoughts about other people. If you're doing that, you're sabotaging the relationship. It's a sign that something's wrong. If you're honestly tempted, or even if you just keep feeling the need to declare your temptation to your partner, then something's going on. You may not be as serious about being in a committed relationship as you thought. Has something changed? Are you getting what you need?

There's a way to approach that conversation with your partner, and it's not by saying, "By the way, I think your co-worker's really hot." You need to bring up the fact that you want to try something new or just discuss you're unhappiness and why you have doubts with the way things are going.

Do: Put yourself in their shoes.

As with many things in life, the Golden Rule applies. What would you want your partner to do in the same situation? Put yourself in their situation before you discuss your temptation with them. That way, you can see and avoid anything that may unnecessarily hurt your partner.

Finances

Ariadna Pérez Hernández

Chapter 6

Finances

In an ideal world, money wouldn't matter with you and your partner. In the real world, unfortunately, we have to deal with lack of funds, disparities between partners, unexpected bills and emergencies. You may commit to a partner that is very wealthy and wants to shower you with material things that could sway your judgment and decisions.

Don't: Let it control your decision.

You should never allow wealth to influence you when committing to a relationship. It will fail in the end. This is not to say that you shouldn't share in the good fortunes of a committed relationship that has financial stability, but the decision to enter into a committed relationship should be made because of compatibility and the emotional connection shared between two people.

The important thing, again, is communication. Don't lie about how much or how little money you have; it shouldn't matter to someone who is in the relationship for you. Honesty is still the best policy. If there's a big disparity between you, make agreements about how much you're allowed to spend together, how expensive your dates can be, etc. Place financial limitations to be on an even footing and so no one feels jealous or left out.

Do: Agree to financial terms.

When it comes to sharing your lives more intimately, your finances are going to become entwined. You have to agree from the start on how you're going to do deal with that. Are you going to give your partner access to your bank accounts, create a separate bank account that the two of you share or keep your finances separate and parcel out the bills? Whatever you do, make sure you're both paying your way equally or at least in such a way that you're happy with the arrangement.

The fact is, only two of people rate wealth as the most important factor in a partner. This figure is from an exclusive study conducted by "DatingAdvice.com," which surveyed respondents over the course of three weeks to get an accurate representation of the U.S. population. Money makes the world go 'round, but how much does it drive our romantic lives? According to the "DatingAdvice.com" study, not very much.

Three percent of men and women aged 25 to 44 picked money as the number one quality, versus just one percent of men and women aged 54 and older. African-Americans had the highest response with five percent, while only one percent of Caucasians answered in the affirmative. Those earning between $100,000 and $124,999 per year were three times as likely to rank money as the highest trait than those earning between $75,000 and $99,999 annually.

Gina Stewart, DatingAdvice.com expert, says that daters generally pair up with someone whose status mirrors their own.

"High-wage earners are statistically more likely to choose wealth as an important factor because wealth plays a great role in their lives," said Gina.

Regionally, the preference was found to be twice as popular in Southern and Western states than in Northeastern and Midwestern states. Perhaps surprisingly, gay men and women were found just as likely as straight respondents to rank wealth as a top quality in a partner, with two percent of each group stating their preferences. There was also no difference detected between participants of varying marital statuses.

Think before you make big decisions. You want to make sure you're in a stable relationship and that you trust your partner before you commit to something huge like becoming a homeowner, going into business together or becoming responsible for any of their prior financial commitments.

Faith

Ariadna Pérez Hernández

Chapter 7

Faith

You don't have to share your partner's faith, but you do have to acknowledge that widely differing views could be a problem. Older generation's faith was a nonstarter with many long-term relationships. Often, depending on the faith, couples were not allowed to marry outside of their religion. That meant one of the partners would have to compromise their faith in order to enter into a committed relationship.

In the 21st century there's no reason for faith to come between you as long as you respect your partner's views and they respect yours. It can be nice to have a relationship with someone who shares your beliefs and your approach to life, sex, marriage, children, etc. It can be just as nice to have someone who challenges your ideas and broadens your horizons with their differences, not to mention sharing the similar views that different faiths have in common.

Don't: Be disrespectful.

If you're not respectful of your partner's beliefs, you can't expect them to respect your faith. It's important to have an open discussion about why you don't respect your partner's faith prior to entering into a committed relationship.

In Margarita Tartavosky's article, "7 Ways To Make Interfaith Relationships Work," an interesting quote about how people deal with interfaith relationships stands out:

"People try to minimize the differences when they're in love," says Joel Crohn, Ph.D., author of *Mixed Matches: How to Create Successful Interracial, Interethnic and Interfaith Relationships.*

Margarita Tartavosky, M.S., taking this quote into consideration, adds the following:

"But dismissing the differences can be detrimental to a couple in the future. If you're part of an interfaith relationship, you have an extra layer of diversity to deal with."

Crohn's book has a lot of good interfaith relationship advice. Here are some of the best pieces:

1. Face the issues.

Again, the biggest problem facing interfaith couples is denying that differences actually exist. Even if you're not that religious, differences can creep up in the future," says Crohn.

Also, in avoiding a dialogue about differences, couples might make inaccurate assumptions about their partner's religious preferences. (Interestingly, "people tend to become more religious with age," according to Crohn.)

2. Clarify your cultural code.

"People have trouble separating religion and culture," says Crohn. Even if religion isn't a factor in your life or your relationship (e.g., you're both agnostic), you still have different cultural codes than your partner. And these differences, he says, don't disappear.

3. Clarify your identity.

Many interfaith couples will start negotiating what religion they want their kids to be without having a clear idea of their own identity. It's common for "members of minority groups in America…to have a complicated sense of their own identity," says Crohn. Self-exploration is key!

Faith

4. Practice "unconditional experimentation."

It's also not productive to negotiate "until you've exposed yourself to your partner's religious practices," says Crohn. Doing so allows a greater understanding of your partner.

5. Share your histories with each other.

Instead of forcing a decision (e.g., "we'll have this type of wedding" or "our son will be raised Catholic"), Crohn encourages couples to discuss their religious and cultural experiences with each other. Not only does this take the pressure off, but it gives couples the opportunity to get to know each other better.

6. Consider a course.

Today, there are many courses for relationships that can help couples resolve a variety of issues. One place that has a variety of resources is www.smartmarriages.com. Crohn cautions readers to be discerning consumers and to look for courses that are skills-based, time-limited and inexpensive.

7. View therapy as preventative.

Couples typically wait until their relationship has suffered before they seek counseling. Crohn encourages readers to see a therapist before getting to this state. Be proactive. He suggests interviewing the therapist to make sure that they can help with your concerns.

When it comes to faith, family can get in the way. Your religiously conservative family might have a big problem with you having a liberal pagan for a partner. The important thing is to listen to their concerns, but tell them firmly that this is your decision to make and that you would like them to welcome your partner to the family with the same warmth they would have for anyone else. If they can't accept your decision, and respect your choices and beliefs, then you need to have some serious discussions about boundaries.

Family

Ariadna Pérez Hernández

Chapter 8

Family

Since we're speaking of family... there are a lot of issues that can come up in this area. Your parents can like or dislike your partner, your sibling might like your partner a bit too much and that's before you even start worrying about what their family thinks of you. The decision to have children, how many and when also comes into play during long-term, committed relationships.

Whatever happens, your families are going to have opinions on the relationship and it's really up to you on how much you allow this to affect your behavior. It's always going to be rude to break the rules in your parents' house and it'll pay to respect them in that context, but once you're out from under their roof, they have no right to lay down the law.

Don't: Let your family take control.

It's best if you can stay friendly with your family and your partner's family and have their support, but they're not in charge of your life. Don't let them try to be.

Do: Prioritize your relationship.

As someone in a committed, long-term relationship, your responsibility is now to your partner before anyone else. Your partner's family may try and intrude too much and that's something you're going to have to talk to your partner about. Agree on an approach and be firm – resist the urge to annoy your mother and father-in-law, even when it's fun.

Studies have shown that if your partner has a strong relationship with your family, the risk of divorce or separation is reduced by twenty percent: it's worth it to make sure everyone gets along. This figure was found in "Husband's Relationship with In-Laws Decreases Risk of Divorce by 20 Percent" "C. Price, 12/02/12."

Though popular culture will have you believe it's a social law that men don't like their wife's family, in reality, that's not always the case. Some men get along with their in-laws much better than others and a husband's choice to develop that relationship dramatically decreases the chance of a divorce, according to a recent study.

The results of the study couldn't have been any more conclusive. Starting in 1986, Terri Orbuch, psychology and research professor at the University of Michigan tracked 373 couples over the first year of their marriage and periodically checked in with them.

Now, 26 years later, Orbuch has compiled her research and found a number of interesting conclusions about what makes one marriage work and another marriage fail, not least of which is the positive role of a man's relationship with his in-laws.

"A close relationship between a husband and his wife's parents results in a much lower risk of divorce–but not the other way around."

Oddly enough, while a man's close relationship with his in-laws increases the chance of marriage survival by twenty percent, a woman's relationship with her in-laws runs in the opposite direction. Orbuch found that women who had close relationships with their husband's parents had a twenty percent greater chance of divorce. Orbuch hypothesized this was because women may consider their in-law's opinions to be "meddling, while men are more interested in providing for their families and take their in-law's actions less personally."

Women are also more likely to value a man's attempts to bond with her parents more than her husband would value her similar actions, according to Elizabeth Bernstein, a columnist at the *Wall Street Journal*. Bernstein says that when a woman sees her husband bonding with her parents, she feels that "he cares about me if he's going to bother with my parents. If he's going to take care of my parents…he really cares about me."

Friends

Ariadna Pérez Hernández

Chapter 9

Friends

The foundation of any committed relationship is based on friendship; many relationships begin with the heat of emotions, but after spending time with that person you find out that you are not compatible as friends.

Do: Evaluate how you feel about each other as friends before committing to a relationship.

The worst thing you can do when entering a relationship is to drop all your friends and spend all your time with your partner. You need other people around for support, to keep life interesting, to invite to the wedding, ask to be godparents or to drive you to the hospital at 3 a.m. after your partner has had a car accident (well, I hope not). It might be good to keep some separate interests and friends, or any rough patches might leave one or both of you without any support.

Don't: Go to extremes with friends.

Partners should not spend too much time with their partner's friends. This could lead to uncomfortable situations do to interpolate motives by friends. Studies suggest that this has led to the break up of committed relationships more often than any other reason. On the other hand, it sends some very bad signals when you won't introduce your partner to your friends. If there are issues, it's best to talk it out!

If you've got a friend you know your partner won't approve of, you don't have to turn them into best buddies, you just need to make sure that you respect your partner's feelings and don't do anything silly like sneaking around behind their back just to see a friend you think they're uncomfortable with.

And if your friends don't like your partner… they may have a point or are just envious of your partner and the time you spend with them. Either way, you need to listen to them, accept their feelings and then work around it so that nobody has to make uncomfortable small talk in your living room!

Sex

Ariadna Pérez Hernández

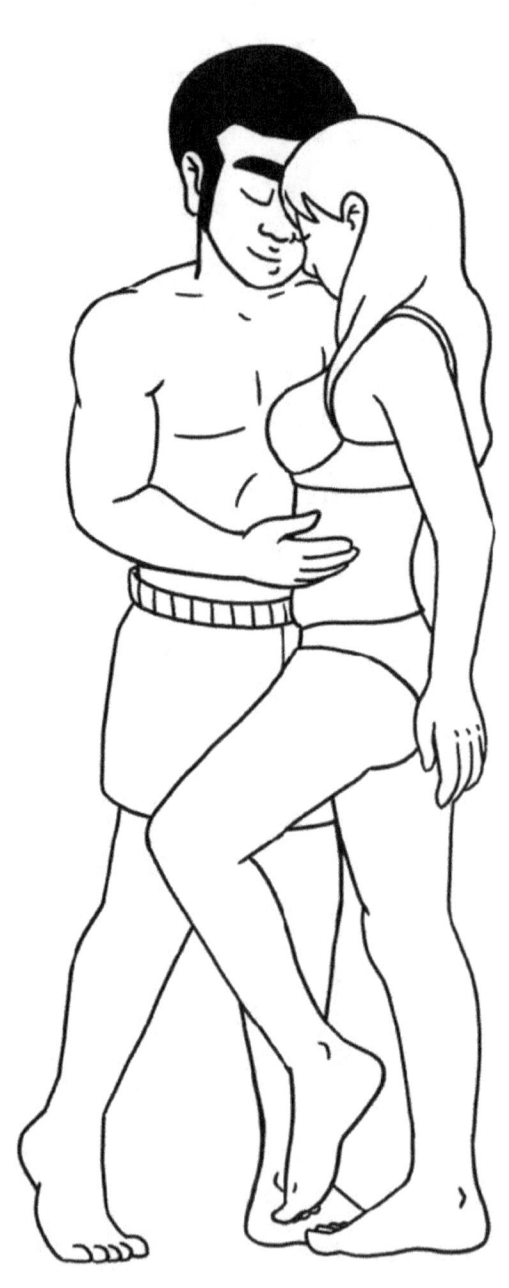

Chapter 10

Sex

Make no mistake about it; sex is one of the most important things in a committed relationship. More relationships fall apart because of sexual dissatisfaction than any other factor. If a partner is dissatisfied with sex in the relationship, they may seek it out in other partners. Many people who have been married for years, have children and stayed married because of their faith and values, but did not enjoy sex with their partner have committed adultery and left the relationship.

Sex has to be important in your relationship if you want it to flourish. In the modern era, more couples have made the decision to live together to get to know each other more intimately prior to marriage. Even if you're not planning to have sex yet and you're pretty sure your partner's on the same page, it's a good idea to talk about it. It may feel awkward, but you're sharing your life with someone and this is part of it. Make sure you both know what's going on so there are no misunderstandings, like worries about whether you really find your partner attractive or vice versa.

If there's something you're not satisfied with in your sex life, again, it's important to talk about it. Otherwise, you start resenting your partner for not knowing your concerns, not that they could. They're not a mind reader; how could they? Even if you want something kind of out there and you're not sure your partner will go for it, it's better to talk about it. You might be surprised and that kind of emotional intimacy can really help your relationship in general. The really important thing is to stick to any ground rules the two of you may have. If you're in an exclusive, longterm relationship, act like it. Don't go off and sleep with someone else. Don't laugh about your partner's skills in bed behind their back. Don't make it all about what you want and ignore what they want.

If you're unsure of what to do, and you haven't discussed it, it's pretty common to have problems making the transition between abstinence and intimacy.

OREM — A pilot study about making the transition from abstinence to sexual intimacy after marriage says that 56% of individuals did not talk about the marriage night beforehand. The pilot looked at individuals who had practiced abstinence before marriage and their transition to marital intimacy. Of the anonymous participants, 91% were members of The Church of Jesus Christ of Latter-day Saints who had been married on average for 12.3 years. They reported receiving mostly an abstinence-only sex education.

Study author Jeremy Boden, Ph.D., CFLE and full-time faculty of family studies at Utah Valley University, along with researchers Dr. Nate Cottle and Joyce Starks found that many individuals who struggled with the transition also had a lack of sexual knowledge.

When asked if they had received a "sex talk" with their parents or guardian, 53% responded in the affirmative, 33% said no and 14% were not sure. Of the participants, 73% were taught abstinence-only sex education. 28% were taught about human sexual response.

"People talked about how they just didn't have enough sexual knowledge going into the relationship. They didn't know what they were doing. They had this inadequate knowledge," Boden said. "One person said it was like two blind people discussing a painting. They didn't have any knowledge to pull from."

Before marriage, only 44% talked about their wedding night with their future partner, 83% talked about birth control and 87% talked about family planning. The numbers regarding communication with non-married couples about the specifics of sex, including individual sexual boundaries, frequency or turning down sex were 32% and below.

Often, Boden said, these unhealthy sexual scripts led to uncertainness or unrealistic expectations about the actual act. Sexual knowledge, healthy sexual scripts, emotional safety and sexual communication, however, were main factors in creating sexual security and healthy relationships.

"If I have the knowledge, then I have healthy knowledge about sex. If I feel safe in this relationship — if I feel good in this relationship — then I'm going to feel safe to talk about it," Boden said. "If those things are going on before marriage, and I would say after marriage, then we have this sexual security and people feel comfortable and safe about talking about it."

[Struggles from abstinence to intimacy after marriage are common, study says]

In the article "6 (Other) Great Things Sex Can Do For You] (Talking About Sex During Sex Is Good for Sex" by Stephanie Pappas, study researcher Elizabeth Babin says, "How people talk about sex is an important topic for public health researchers. After all, people who are uncomfortable asking their partners to wear a condom may be at higher risk of having unprotected sex and exposing themselves to sexually transmitted infections. Communication is a key to having enjoyable sexual encounters."

According to Babin, little research has delved into what keeps people from talking about their likes and dislikes while in bed.

"In order to increase communication quality, we need to figure out why people are communicating and why they're not communicating," said Babin. To do so, Babin recruited 207 people, 88 from undergraduate classes and 119 from online sites, to complete surveys about their apprehension to sexual communication, their sexual satisfaction and the amount of non-verbal and verbal communication they felt they engaged in during sex.

For example, participants were asked how much they agreed with statements such as, "I feel nervous when I think about talking to my partner about the sexual aspects of our relationship," and "I feel anxious when I think about telling my partner what I dislike during sex."

The participants, whose average age was 29, also responded to questions about their sexual self-esteem, such as how good a partner they felt they were and how confident they were in their sexual skills.

Getting comfortable with communicating about sex may translate to benefits in the bedroom, especially if the lines of communication are open during the act. New research finds that comfort with sexual communication is directly linked to sexual satisfaction. Nonetheless, this difference doesn't completely explain why the sexually chatty are happier with their erotic lives.

"Even if you just have a little bit of anxiety about the communication, that affects whether you're communicating or not, but it also directly affects their satisfaction," said study researcher Elizabeth Babin, an expert on health communication at Cleveland State University in Ohio. The anxiety "might be kind of taking them out of the moment and therefore reducing the overall satisfaction they experience during their encounters,"

Politics
Ariadna Pérez Hernández

Chapter 11

Politics

Like religion, this is a topic that can divide people pretty sharply. My advice here is the opposite from the faith chapter: you don't have to talk about it. Obviously, if you're completely opposed on major issues, you may not be as compatible with your partner as you hoped. But if that's the case and you still want to be with that person, you don't have to discuss politics. Just agree with your partner that it's a topic that's out of bounds and stick to that, no matter how tempting it is.

Even if you disagree with your partner's politics, it is important to support them in having those views, voting for people who will further their cause or even campaigning themselves. You don't have to agree with them to let them know that you'll always have their back and if you try and sabotage them, you're definitely not being a good partner.

Of course, you may enjoy having political debates with your partner, whether you agree or not. Whatever works for you is great, just keep in mind that you love this person and want to be with them, so calling them names might not be the best policy.

Conclusion

After reading my advice, you'll probably conclude that it comes down to variations of the first two points: honesty and communication. Be your best self with your partner, make sure they know what's going on in your mind, especially if it might cause problems, and remember to respect them wherever there might be a conflict. You don't have to agree with your partner all the time, as long as you're emotionally available to support them and let them know that you love them no matter what they believe in. Explore Notes-Partners Relationship Log, a perfect way to commutate intimately at the end of this book.

And finally, a piece of advice from my father: if two people live together or share their lives in some way and claim they never argue or disagree, they're lying and/or kidding themselves. Conflicts and disagreements happen, it's the way you work through them, and that matters.

Contributors Research Sources

Contributing Writer
Uzma Batool

Research Sources Cited
[Talking About Sex During Sex Is Good for Sex]
Stephanie Pappas, Live Science Senior Writer, September 05, 2012
http://www.livescience.com/22934-talking-about-sex-satisfaction.html
[Live Science. "Other Great Things Sex Can Do For You]

Jeremy Boden, Ph.D., CFLE, Dr. Nate Cottle, Joyce Starks Babin, September 05, 2012
http://www.livescience.com/22934-talking-about-sex-satisfaction.html
[Perceptions of Partner Sexual Satisfaction in Heterosexual Committed Relationships]

Erin E. Fallis, Uzma S. Rehman, Christine Purdon
April 2014, Volume 43, Issue 3, pp. 541-550 Date: 29 Aug 2013
[http://link.springer.com/article/10.1007/s10508-013-0177-y#page-1
[Only 2% of Americans Rank Wealth as the Most Important Partner Quality]

C. Price • 2/11/14
http://www.datingadvice.com/studies/o2oarw
[Struggles from abstinence to intimacy after marriage common, study says]

By Celeste Tholen Rosenlof, November 13th, 2013
http://www.ksl.com/?nid=1010&sid=27617437

[7 Ways To Make Interfaith Relationships Work} MARGARITA TARTAKOVSKY, M.S.

October 23, 2013

http://psychcentral.com/lib/7-ways-to-make-interfaith-relationships-work/0006977

"Straight from the Heart by Layne and Paul Cutright] May, 7, 2011
http://lifeesteem.org/wellness/wellness_truth.html

[Husband's Relationship with In-Laws Decreases Risk of Divorce by 20 Percent]

C. Price, 12/02/12
http://www.datingadvice.com/studies/hcrid

[Tolerance, An Important Relationship Virtue]
Sonja Ridden, OCTOBER 12, 2011
http://www.healthyrelationshipsmatter.com/2011/10/tolerance-important-relationship-virtue.html
[Practicing tolerance is one key to a healthy relationship]

LOIS ROTHSCHILD, Oct. 26, 2011, Updated Aug. 21, 2013
http://www.ocregister.com/articles/cloke-323854-talk-don.html

About Notes-Partners Relationship Log

This section of the book is about strengthening and rejuvenating the caring relationship between partners. In relationships partners often hesitate to discuss sensitive things Face To Face and are unlikely to share anything about each other and themselves for that matter.

The Author of this book created this section so as to encourage reader's with partners to post remarks, comments, answers or whatever they want to share with their partner in simple note form. The notes allow for partners to become more loving towards each other and in essence become a unit rather than just mare people in a Committed Relationships.

Communication is the key foundation for any strong relationship and the Notes provide a vessel that channels those discussions.

Keep in mind that you have to approach this communication tool with an open mind and willingness to communicate and trust each other no matter what the other writes. The Notes are only available in the book's paperback version. Take A Look At Samples of Notes-Partner Relationship Logs Below

Name: Bob
Date: Monday
Time: Lunch
Mood: Horny
Comments: I really miss seeing you in your sexy lingerie. You are still hot and I miss the show.

Name: Mary
Date: 7/1
Time: 3PM
Mood: Happy
Comments: I miss it too, it is just that after I had the baby I did not feel sexy anymore and I simply forgot that I had such things around. I will pull them out soon, so be prepared for the show of a lifetime and expect to see the hot me once again.

Name: Mary
Date: 7/7
Time: 8PM
Mood: Wondering
Comments: hey honey, I wanted to let you know that I am really jealous of your new secretary and I thought you should know. Saying it here also felt like the right thing to do so as to avoid loads of accusations and assumptions.

Name: Bob
Date: 7/7
Time: 10PM
Mood: Smiley face
Comments: What! You should have no worries there, as my eyes are only for you and you alone. Even the guys at work often look at you all the time saying how luckier I am to have you.

Name: Mary
Date: 7/7
Time: Midnight
Mood: Blessed
Comments: I love you so much honey! And thank you for loving me too... guys at work looking at me??? Now that is a shocker... Ha! Ha! Ha!

Name: Mary
Date: 7/10
Time: 11 AM
Mood: Kisses
Comments: Hi honey, thanks very much for taking me dancing last night. I had so much fun with you, it really brought up some old memories we have had. Thanks again, love you

Start Getting Closer Leave Notes Below

Name:

Date:

Time:

Mood:

Comments:

Name:

Date:

Time:

Mood:

Comments:

Name:

Date:

Time:

Mood:

Comments:

Name:

Date:

Time:

Mood:

Comments:

Name:
Date:
Time:
Mood:
Comments:

Name:
Date:
Time:
Mood:
Comments:

Name:
Date:
Time:
Mood:
Comments:

Name:
Date:
Time:
Mood:
Comments:

Name:

Date:

Time:

Mood:

Comments:

Name:

Date:

Time:

Mood:

Comments:

Name:

Date:

Time:

Mood:

Comments:

Name:

Date:

Time:

Mood:

Comments:

Name:
Date:
Time:
Mood:
Comments:

Name:
Date:
Time:
Mood:
Comments:

Name:
Date:
Time:
Mood:
Comments:

Name:
Date:
Time:
Mood:
Comments:

Name:
Date:
Time:
Mood:
Comments:

Name:
Date:
Time:
Mood:
Comments:

Name:
Date:
Time:
Mood:
Comments:

Name:
Date:
Time:
Mood:
Comments:

Name:

Date:

Time:

Mood:

Comments:

Name:

Date:

Time:

Mood:

Comments:

Name:

Date:

Time:

Mood:

Comments:

Name:

Date:

Time:

Mood:

Comments:

Notes-Partners Relationship Log

Name:

Date:

Time:

Mood:

Comments:

Name:

Date:

Time:

Mood:

Comments:

Name:

Date:

Time:

Mood:

Comments:

Name:

Date:

Time:

Mood:

Comments:

Name:

Date:

Time:

Mood:

Comments:

Name:

Date:

Time:

Mood:

Comments:

Name:

Date:

Time:

Mood:

Comments:

Name:

Date:

Time:

Mood:

Comments:

Notes-Partners Relationship Log

Name:
Date:
Time:
Mood:
Comments:

Name:
Date:
Time:
Mood:
Comments:

Name:
Date:
Time:
Mood:
Comments:

Name:
Date:
Time:
Mood:
Comments:

Name:

Date:

Time:

Mood:

Comments:

Name:

Date:

Time:

Mood:

Comments:

Name:

Date:

Time:

Mood:

Comments:

Name:

Date:

Time:

Mood:

Comments:

Notes-Partners Relationship Log

Name:
Date:
Time:
Mood:
Comments:

Name:
Date:
Time:
Mood:
Comments:

Name:
Date:
Time:
Mood:
Comments:

Name:
Date:
Time:
Mood:
Comments:

Name:
Date:
Time:
Mood:
Comments:

Name:
Date:
Time:
Mood:
Comments:

Name:
Date:
Time:
Mood:
Comments:

Name:
Date:
Time:
Mood:
Comments:

Name:

Date:

Time:

Mood:

Comments:

Name:

Date:

Time:

Mood:

Comments:

Name:

Date:

Time:

Mood:

Comments:

Name:

Date:

Time:

Mood:

Comments:

Name:

Date:

Time:

Mood:

Comments:

Name:

Date:

Time:

Mood:

Comments:

Name:

Date:

Time:

Mood:

Comments:

Name:

Date:

Time:

Mood:

Comments:

Name:
Date:
Time:
Mood:
Comments:

Name:
Date:
Time:
Mood:
Comments:

Name:
Date:
Time:
Mood:
Comments:

Name:
Date:
Time:
Mood:
Comments:

Name:
Date:
Time:
Mood:
Comments:

Name:
Date:
Time:
Mood:
Comments:

Name:
Date:
Time:
Mood:
Comments:

Name:
Date:
Time:
Mood:
Comments:

Name:

Date:

Time:

Mood:

Comments:

Name:

Date:

Time:

Mood:

Comments:

Name:

Date:

Time:

Mood:

Comments:

Name:

Date:

Time:

Mood:

Comments:

Name:

Date:

Time:

Mood:

Comments:

Name:

Date:

Time:

Mood:

Comments:

Name:

Date:

Time:

Mood:

Comments:

Name:

Date:

Time:

Mood:

Comments:

Notes-Partners Relationship Log

Name:

Date:

Time:

Mood:

Comments:

Name:

Date:

Time:

Mood:

Comments:

Name:

Date:

Time:

Mood:

Comments:

Name:

Date:

Time:

Mood:

Comments:

Name:
Date:
Time:
Mood:
Comments:

Name:
Date:
Time:
Mood:
Comments:

Name:
Date:
Time:
Mood:
Comments:

Name:
Date:
Time:
Mood:
Comments:

Notes-Partners Relationship Log

Name:
Date:
Time:
Mood:
Comments:

Name:
Date:
Time:
Mood:
Comments:

Name:
Date:
Time:
Mood:
Comments:

Name:
Date:
Time:
Mood:
Comments:

Name:
Date:
Time:
Mood:
Comments:

Name:
Date:
Time:
Mood:
Comments:

Name:
Date:
Time:
Mood:
Comments:

Name:
Date:
Time:
Mood:
Comments:

Notes-Partners Relationship Log

Name:
Date:
Time:
Mood:
Comments:

Name:
Date:
Time:
Mood:
Comments:

Name:
Date:
Time:
Mood:
Comments:

Name:
Date:
Time:
Mood:
Comments:

Name:
Date:
Time:
Mood:
Comments:

Name:
Date:
Time:
Mood:
Comments:

Name:
Date:
Time:
Mood:
Comments:

Name:
Date:
Time:
Mood:
Comments:

Notes-Partners Relationship Log

Name:
Date:
Time:
Mood:
Comments:

Name:
Date:
Time:
Mood:
Comments:

Name:
Date:
Time:
Mood:
Comments:

Name:
Date:
Time:
Mood:
Comments:

Name:
Date:
Time:
Mood:
Comments:

Name:
Date:
Time:
Mood:
Comments:

Name:
Date:
Time:
Mood:
Comments:

Name:
Date:
Time:
Mood:
Comments:

Notes-Partners Relationship Log

Name:
Date:
Time:
Mood:
Comments:

Name:
Date:
Time:
Mood:
Comments:

Name:
Date:
Time:
Mood:
Comments:

Name:
Date:
Time:
Mood:
Comments:

Name:
Date:
Time:
Mood:
Comments:

Name:
Date:
Time:
Mood:
Comments:

Name:
Date:
Time:
Mood:
Comments:

Name:
Date:
Time:
Mood:
Comments:

Name:

Date:

Time:

Mood:

Comments:

Name:

Date:

Time:

Mood:

Comments:

Name:

Date:

Time:

Mood:

Comments:

Name:

Date:

Time:

Mood:

Comments:

Name:

Date:

Time:

Mood:

Comments:

Name:

Date:

Time:

Mood:

Comments:

Name:

Date:

Time:

Mood:

Comments:

Name:

Date:

Time:

Mood:

Comments:

Name:

Date:

Time:

Mood:

Comments:

Name:

Date:

Time:

Mood:

Comments:

Name:

Date:

Time:

Mood:

Comments:

Name:

Date:

Time:

Mood:

Comments:

Name:

Date:

Time:

Mood:

Comments:

Name:

Date:

Time:

Mood:

Comments:

Name:

Date:

Time:

Mood:

Comments:

Name:

Date:

Time:

Mood:

Comments:

Name:
Date:
Time:
Mood:
Comments:

Name:
Date:
Time:
Mood:
Comments:

Name:
Date:
Time:
Mood:
Comments:

Name:
Date:
Time:
Mood:
Comments:

Name:

Date:

Time:

Mood:

Comments:

Name:

Date:

Time:

Mood:

Comments:

Name:

Date:

Time:

Mood:

Comments:

Name:

Date:

Time:

Mood:

Comments:

Name:
Date:
Time:
Mood:
Comments:

Name:
Date:
Time:
Mood:
Comments:

Name:
Date:
Time:
Mood:
Comments:

Name:
Date:
Time:
Mood:
Comments:

Name:

Date:

Time:

Mood:

Comments:

Name:

Date:

Time:

Mood:

Comments:

Name:

Date:

Time:

Mood:

Comments:

Name:

Date:

Time:

Mood:

Comments:

Name:

Date:

Time:

Mood:

Comments:

Name:

Date:

Time:

Mood:

Comments:

Name:

Date:

Time:

Mood:

Comments:

Name:

Date:

Time:

Mood:

Comments:

Name:

Date:

Time:

Mood:

Comments:

Name:

Date:

Time:

Mood:

Comments:

Name:

Date:

Time:

Mood:

Comments:

Name:

Date:

Time:

Mood:

Comments:

Notes-Partners Relationship Log

Name:
Date:
Time:
Mood:
Comments:

Name:
Date:
Time:
Mood:
Comments:

Name:
Date:
Time:
Mood:
Comments:

Name:
Date:
Time:
Mood:
Comments:

Name:
Date:
Time:
Mood:
Comments:

Name:
Date:
Time:
Mood:
Comments:

Name:
Date:
Time:
Mood:
Comments:

Name:
Date:
Time:
Mood:
Comments:

Name:

Date:

Time:

Mood:

Comments:

Name:

Date:

Time:

Mood:

Comments:

Name:

Date:

Time:

Mood:

Comments:

Name:

Date:

Time:

Mood:

Comments:

Notes-Partners Relationship Log

Name:
Date:
Time:
Mood:
Comments:

Name:
Date:
Time:
Mood:
Comments:

Name:
Date:
Time:
Mood:
Comments:

Name:
Date:
Time:
Mood:
Comments:

Name:
Date:
Time:
Mood:
Comments:

Name:
Date:
Time:
Mood:
Comments:

Name:
Date:
Time:
Mood:
Comments:

Name:
Date:
Time:
Mood:
Comments:

Name:
Date:
Time:
Mood:
Comments:

Name:
Date:
Time:
Mood:
Comments:

Name:
Date:
Time:
Mood:
Comments:

Name:
Date:
Time:
Mood:
Comments:

Name:
Date:
Time:
Mood:
Comments:

Name:
Date:
Time:
Mood:
Comments:

Name:
Date:
Time:
Mood:
Comments:

Name:
Date:
Time:
Mood:
Comments:

Name:

Date:

Time:

Mood:

Comments:

Name:

Date:

Time:

Mood:

Comments:

Name:

Date:

Time:

Mood:

Comments:

Name:

Date:

Time:

Mood:

Comments:

Notes-Partners Relationship Log

Name:

Date:

Time:

Mood:

Comments:

Name:

Date:

Time:

Mood:

Comments:

Name:

Date:

Time:

Mood:

Comments:

Name:

Date:

Time:

Mood:

Comments:

Now that you have shared notes in this book and after reading, the next step you want to do is set down together and read all of the notes you both wrote from the start. All the Notes emotions you shared over time and how you intimately expressed those emotions will bring you closer together as you reread them.

It Just Works That Way; To Continue Growing and Loving Together, You Can Purchase Notes-Partner Relationship Log, 100 Page Log Book at www.houstonepublishing

www.ingramcontent.com/pod-product-compliance
Lightning Source LLC
Chambersburg PA
CBHW072056290426
44110CB00014B/1698